S0-EKO-998

Snowy Owl
AT HOME ON THE TUNDRA

WRITTEN BY SARAH TOAST
ILLUSTRATED BY KEVIN TORLINE

Publications International, Ltd.

The long winter's snow
is just beginning to melt away
as Mother Snowy Owl scrapes
a shallow nest on top of a very
small hill. In spring it is cold
on the Arctic tundra.

The ground is still wet, so
Mother Owl lines the nest with
moss and feathers. She settles
into the nest, then she calls to
Father Snowy Owl.

Mother Owl lays a glossy white egg in the nest and sits on top of it, sharing the warmth of her body with the egg. Father Owl brings a lemming for Mother Owl to eat. He brings her food so she doesn't have to leave the nest.

The next day, Mother Owl lays another white egg, and two days after that another, until there are eight eggs in the nest.

The springtime wildflowers bloom bright as Mother Owl sits patiently on the nest. She and Father Owl call to each other to keep in touch.

As the long spring days pass, Father Owl makes many flights to hunt for lemmings and hares. He flies swiftly and silently. Father Owl brings back meals caught in his sharp claws. XX

Lemmings are mouse-size animals that burrow beneath the snow in the late fall, winter, and early spring. They come out in the warmer months.

Other tundra animals—arctic foxes and weasels, falcons and hawks—are also hunting for the lemmings. Father Owl competes with foxes and wolves when he hunts for hares. XX

Finally the first tiny owlet hatches out of the first egg laid by Mother Owl. Baby Snowy is covered with soft white down.

As soon as Snowy is able to eat, Father and Mother Owl feed him tender bits they have stored nearby. The next day, another owlet hatches. After ten days, Snowy has seven brothers and sisters.

A caribou wanders too close to the family's nest. Mother and Father Owl shrill "krick-krick, krick-krick" to drive him off. Snowy also tries his hardest to "krick-krick."

The caribou looks up from his grazing. When the caribou turns and wanders away from the nest, Father Owl calls out a loud "ho-ho."

Caribou are visitors to the tundra during the summertime, but shaggy musk oxen live there all year round. Musk oxen and caribou eat the grasses, leaves, and mosses that abound in the long days of summer.

Snowy and his family watch the musk oxen. Like other owls, Snowy can turn his head around to see what's behind him. XX

Snowy and his brothers and sisters are growing bigger daily. Mother Owl no longer covers them in the nest. Mother Owl stands guard near the nest while Father Owl searches for a hare to feed the large family.

During the midsummer, when the Arctic nights are as light as day, Snowy steps out of the nest and spreads his wings. XX

Snowy steps slowly down the small hill. He is the first owlet in the family to climb over the rocks and walk through all of the wildflowers near the nest. He sees a snow goose gliding above him.

Snowy is so happy he hoots. Mother Owl and the owlets look over from the nest to make sure Snowy is safe. ×x